4/10

TEEN LIFE™

FREQUENTLY ASKED QUESTIONS ABOUT

Driving and the Law

Greg
Roza

ROSEN
PUBLISHING®
New York

Published in 2010 by The Rosen Publishing Group, Inc.
29 East 21st Street, New York, NY 10010

Library of Congress Cataloging-in-Publication Data

Roza, Greg.
Frequently asked questions about driving and the law / Greg Roza.—1st ed.
    p. cm.—(FAQ: teen life)
Includes index.
ISBN 978-1-4358-3544-3 (library binding)
1. Automobile driving—United States—Miscellanea. 2. Traffic regulations—United States—Miscellanea. 3. Traffic safety—Miscellanea. I. Title.
TL152.52.R69 2010
629.28'3—dc22

2009013248

Manufactured in Malaysia

CPSIA Compliance Information: Batch #TWW10YA: For Further Information contact Rosen Publishing, New York, New York at 1-800-237-9932

Contents

HOW DO I LEARN TO DRIVE?

Becoming a teenager is an exciting time in your life. The older you get, the more privileges you get. With more privileges, however, come more responsibilities. Teens are expected to be more reliable and conscientious than their younger siblings. Failing to do so may result in their privileges being taken away. Irresponsibility can also lead to disappointed or angry parents, accidents, and injuries to yourself and others. This is especially true when it comes to learning to drive.

Most teens look forward to the day when they can finally get behind the wheel of a car. They're thinking of the freedom and the excitement. But what many of them fail to realize is that driving is a huge responsibility.

You've no doubt been in a car plenty of times while an older person was driving. But have you ever really watched this person's movements or paid attention to his or her eyes and hands? You can learn a lot by observing others and asking questions. Unfortunately, you can't earn a driver's license that way. You need to study, practice, and prove to a state official that you are in fact ready to pilot a vehicle.

Hit the Books

There is a lot you can do to prepare for driving. You can go to your local library or bookstore and ask to see books on driving. Other resources include Web sites and videos. The For More Information section at the back of this book also lists helpful resources.

Perhaps the most important source you can read is a driving manual from your state's Department of Motor Vehicles (DMV). State driving manuals will prepare you for taking your learner's permit test. Many state DMVs will also supply you with practice tests. It's a good idea to read the manual before you even get behind the wheel. Most DMVs have manuals online.

What Is a Learner's Permit?

No matter how much studying you do, you must pass a basic written test and a vision test before you can legally get behind the wheel of a car. Passing these tests will earn you a special license called a learner's permit, also known as a driver's permit. All teens must have the consent of their parent or legal guardian to obtain a permit. The age at which you can

The DMV (Department of Motor Vehicles) is where drivers go to take care of driving-related issues, particularly applying for driver's licenses and registering vehicles.

get your permit and the amount of time it's valid depend on the state.

Learner's permit exams usually have ten to twenty multiple-choice questions. However, the questions that will be asked of you are different than those that another person may be asked. As a result, you need to study the guide and be prepared to answer any questions that may come up. You'll still be able to earn a permit even if you miss one or two questions. You'll have to pay a small fee to take the test, and you can retake the test as many times as you want. Go to your local DMV for more information.

Time to Practice

Once you get your learner's permit, it's time to drive. Don't get too excited just yet. Your first steps—while exciting—should be cautious. Perhaps the most important thing to remember when learning to drive is to be patient. Rushing your instruction is sure to result in potentially dangerous situations. Controlling a hulking mass of steel, glass, and plastic is not something to be taken lightly. In time, driving a car will become second nature to you. However, this will take some time.

It's a good idea to practice with a driver that you trust. Parents are usually the best partners, but an older sibling or family friend may work, too. Many people choose to pay for lessons from a professional driving instructor. Whomever you choose, remember to keep calm, go slowly, and listen to your driving tutor.

When to Practice

Choose a time that's good for both you and your tutor. Nights are a bad choice for the obvious reason of poor visibility. Weekends are a good time because many people are off from school and work. You don't want to be rushed, so make sure you have plenty of time—perhaps an hour a lesson.

Not all of that time should be spent driving. It's also a good idea to learn about the car you're driving, car maintenance, laws, and other important topics related to driving. Also, a few weekends of practice is simply not enough time behind the wheel to sharpen your skills. The time needed will probably differ

There is much to learn about cars and driving after you earn your learner's permit. It's important to have an instructor with you.

depending on the individual. It may take you months of practice before you're ready to take your driving test. Just remember that you have the rest of your life to drive once you get your license, so be patient.

Where to Practice

Inexperienced drivers should never begin practicing on a roadway. In fact, your own driveway might be the best place for your first lesson. It doesn't take a lot of room to learn how to start a car, pull forward, and back up. You can also learn how to change a tire and jump-start a dead battery without leaving the driveway.

When it comes time to learn to brake, turn, speed up, and slow down, an empty parking lot is the best place to practice. It helps to have a few stationary objects to maneuver around, but a wide-open space is best for new drivers.

Once you've become comfortable driving in a parking lot, quiet side streets are ideal areas to put your new skills to the test. It helps to move on to an area that has parked cars, other moving vehicles, and even pedestrians. But the quieter the street, the easier it will be for you to get the hang of road driving. Important techniques to practice on a side street include stopping at intersections, making turns, sharing the road with others, identifying potential dangers, and maintaining an appropriate speed.

After side streets, the next step is to move on to main streets and perhaps highways. These types of roads are usually much busier, faster, and, at times, confusing for a new driver. Don't move off the side streets until you're sure that you can handle it.

It is easier to practice important driving skills in a controlled setting under the guidance of a trained professional.

Drivers Education

Most high schools offer teenagers the opportunity to take a drivers education course, often during the summer months. Also known as drivers ed, this course gives new drivers—often with or without a learner's permit—the chance to learn about driving and the rules of the road in a class of their peers. Drivers ed courses have different areas of concentration, including class lectures, homework and textbooks, and, of course, hands-on driving experience with a trained driving instructor. Some may also make use of driving simulation machines or software. Teens are not required to take drivers ed in order to get a permit or driver's license. However, the instruction you'll receive is invaluable, and it'll help you get lower insurance rates. You can also take an online driver's education course, although you can't get hands-on instruction that way.

Ten Great Questions to Ask a Driving Instructor

1 What is parallel parking, and how do I do it?

2 How do I change a flat tire?

3 How do I jump-start a dead battery?

4 How do I check and change the oil in my car?

5 How do I fill my car with gasoline?

6 What should I keep in my car in case of an emergency?

7 What types of things can distract a driver?

8 What driving skills will I need to learn to pass my driving test?

9 What should I do if I'm ever in a collision?

10 What are blind spots?

chapter two

PREPARING FOR THE ROAD: WHAT DO I DO NOW?

Once you've practiced driving, you will need to prove to a state official that you're ready to drive alone. The road test is the final step in earning your driver's license. This chapter will address key areas that will help prepare you for your road test.

Check the Controls

You should become familiar with your car's gauges and controls, how to operate them, and what they are telling you. Dashboard controls include the lights, emergency lights, windshield wipers, ignition, parking brake, and, in many cars, cruise control. Gauges monitor things like gas, oil, and engine heat. Most cars have lights that tell the driver when there is something wrong with the engine, airbags, doors, brakes, and other parts.

The dashboards of cars today have controls and gauges, some of which you won't be familiar with.

Don't forget to adjust and fasten your seatbelt every time you get behind the wheel. You may also want to adjust the seat, headrest, mirrors, and steering wheel. It's difficult and danger-ous to adjust these things while you are driving, which is when you should be concentrating on the road.

You also want to check the space around the car before getting in and starting the engine. Walk around the car to make sure there are no objects, animals, or people in the way. Bend down to look under the car, which is a place where balls may roll or animals may hide. Check for signs of damage, including fluids, glass, or bolts.

Blind Spots

Vehicles have at least three mirrors to help drivers see without having to take their eyes off the road. However, even with mirrors there are two significant blind spots to the left rear and right rear of the driver. When changing lanes, backing up, and turning, drivers must turn their heads to see if there are any obstructions in these blind spots. Collisions happen when drivers forget to do so, especially when changing lanes on the highway. At first, you may tend to veer in the direction you're turning, rather than keeping the steering wheel straight. When you have enough practice, turning to check your blind spots will become second nature.

Backing Up

Driving in reverse is usually needed for getting in and out of parking spaces or driveways. You won't need to drive in reverse for long distances. Always check your mirrors before and while backing up.

Press down on the brake before putting the car in reverse. Before taking your foot off the brake, place your right arm over the back of your seat, turn to look over your right shoulder, and grip the top of the steering wheel with your left hand. Ease your foot off of the brake. Go slowly—you may not need to step on the accelerator. It's always wise to back up slowly because it's more difficult to see obstructions when you're going backward. As when checking your blind spots, you may have difficulty going

Drivers need to develop the habit of checking their mirrors frequently while driving. Make sure you adjust them before starting the car each time you go out for a drive.

in a straight line at first. It will take a little practice to get the hang of steering while backing up, which is another good reason to take it slowly.

Braking and Accelerating

New drivers often have trouble learning how much force to use when accelerating and braking a car. The pedals can seem sensitive at first, but it doesn't take long to get used to them. Make sure you've had enough practice accelerating and decelerating before taking your driving test. Learn how to avoid abrupt stops and starts.

Sometimes, it's necessary to brake quickly. However, if you know that you'll need to brake up ahead (at a stop sign or red light, for instance), take your foot off of the accelerator about half a block away and allow the car's weight to slow itself. Start braking as you approach the stop. The closer you get to your stop, the more pressure you should put on the brake. Come to a complete stop about a car's length before the stop sign or traffic light.

Many drivers start forward quickly after coming to a stop. This is sometimes called a jackrabbit start. Not only is this bad for your vehicle, but it's also dangerous. You need to be on the lookout for pedestrians and irresponsible drivers who may try to make it through an intersection just as or after the light has turned red. Once you know that the way is clear, ease down on the gas pedal and inch forward. Slowly pick up speed once you're sure it is safe. Gradually accelerate to a safe, legal speed.

Steering and Turning

During your driving test, you'll be graded on your control of the vehicle during turns. Don't turn the steering wheel if the car isn't in motion. This can damage the car.

To understand how to grip the steering wheel, imagine that it is a clock face. Place your hands at the ten o'clock and two o'clock (some sources recommend nine o'clock and three o'clock) positions. To execute a right turn, grip the wheel with your right hand and pull it down to five o'clock while sliding your left hand down to seven o'clock. Then grip the wheel with your left hand and move it back up to ten o'clock to keep turning the vehicle. Repeat these movements until you are halfway through the turn. Then reverse the movements and return the steering wheel to its original position. To execute a left turn, grip the wheel with your left hand and pull it down to seven o'clock while sliding your right hand down to five o'clock. Then grip the wheel with your right hand and move it back up to two o'clock.

Using this style, your hands won't cross over the top of the steering wheel. Some sources recommend crossing the hands over the top while turning. With the use of airbags, however, this style has been deemed unsafe. Other sources recommend releasing the wheel halfway through the turn and allowing it to spin freely back to its original position. This, too, is dangerous because the driver isn't in complete control.

Use Your Signals

Some drivers forget to use their turn signals. Responsible and safe drivers use them every time they make a turn or change lanes. Failing to do so can cause confusion and collisions. It can also cause you to fail your driving test.

You might be required to use hand signals to indicate your turns and stops during a driving test. These are the same hand signals used when riding a bicycle. Extend your left arm out straight to indicate a left turn. Bend your elbow and hold your

Using cones instead of actual cars for your first attempts at parallel parking will help you gain confidence quickly.

hand straight up for a right turn. Bend your elbow and hold your hand straight down to indicate a stop.

What Is Parallel Parking?

Parallel parking is necessary when you need to park in a space on a street between two other vehicles. Even if you don't plan to park on a street where many other people park, you'll need to demonstrate this skill in order to pass your road test. Careful and controlled parallel parking helps show a driving examiner that you know how to handle a car. Many people panic when it comes to parallel parking, but there's no need to when you know how to do it correctly.

Parallel parking includes several key driving techniques, including backing up, judging distances, and using your mirrors. When you do it correctly, the car should perform a smooth, uninterrupted S-turn into the parking spot. It's also usually less trouble than trying to pull into the space front first. When you see an empty space ahead, use your turning signal to tell other drivers that you intend to park. While checking your mirrors for traffic, pedestrians, and obstructions, slowly pull up next to the car in front of the space. When you come to a stop, you should be even with and parallel to the other car, 2 to 3 feet (0.6 to 0.9 meters) away. You may need to wait with your turn signal on for other drivers to go around you.

When the road is clear, push down on the brake and put the car in reverse. Ease up on the brake and back up slowly. When your backseat is about even with the other car's back bumper, turn the wheel hard right and ease slowly into the turn. Watch the back bumper of the other car to avoid hitting it. If your tire hits the curb, pull out a few feet and try again.

Once your car is at a 45-degree angle to the street, turn the wheel hard left while continuing to back up. This will complete the S-turn and bring your front end into the parking spot. Be careful not to back up into the car behind you. To finish, brake the car, place the car in drive, and inch forward as you straighten the wheel. Pull forward until your car is centered in the spot and place the car in park. The tires should be 10 to 12 inches (25 to

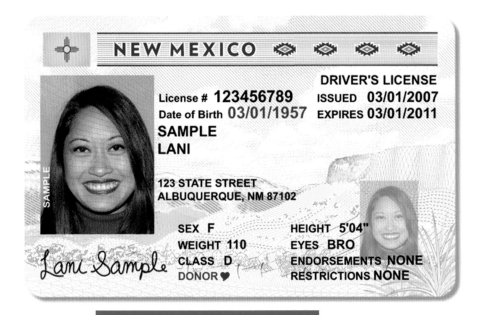

NEW MEXICO

DRIVER'S LICENSE
License # 123456789   ISSUED 03/01/2007
Date of Birth 03/01/1957   EXPIRES 03/01/2011
SAMPLE
LANI

123 STATE STREET
ALBUQUERQUE, NM 87102

SEX F   HEIGHT 5'04"
WEIGHT 110   EYES BRO
CLASS D   ENDORSEMENTS NONE
DONOR ♥   RESTRICTIONS NONE

In addition to being mandatory for driving, a driver's license is an important form of personal identification.

30 centimeters) from the curb. To get out of a parking space, back up, turn the wheel hard left, and pull forward after checking for traffic and pedestrians.

Your Driver's License

Once you pass your road test, you will (finally) earn your driver's license. It displays a picture of you, as well as your weight, height, and eye and hair color. It will also have your birth date, address, and your own identification (ID) number.

Most states today require teens to first obtain a graduated driver's license (GDL). Teens with GDLs need to prove that they are safe, responsible drivers before they can obtain a regular license. Most states require teen drivers to have a clean driving record for one year before GDL restrictions are removed. GDL rules usually include the following conditions:

- A period of adult supervision
- Driving time restrictions (e.g., 5 AM to 10 PM); exceptions include driving to or from work, school functions, childcare, and other responsible activities
- Passenger limitations (e.g., only one passenger under twenty-one years old)
- Mandatory seatbelts for all passengers
- GDL extensions for traffic violations

Driving statistics show there is a good chance that teen drivers will be involved in a collision during their first year of driving. GDL programs have reduced the number of collisions, injuries, and deaths caused by and involving teen drivers.

three

WHAT ARE THE RULES OF THE ROAD?

Traffic laws differ from state to state, but they all have the same motive in mind: safety. All states have simple laws regarding things like littering. Obviously, throwing garbage out of a moving car is dangerous. It is also rude, since you're making others look at and clean up your mess. This is just one example of why we have laws, including driving laws, and why it's important for people to follow them.

In South Dakota, you can get a driver's license when you turn fourteen. But you must be seventeen to get one in New Jersey. Legal driving ages in the rest of the states fall between these ages. As mentioned in the previous chapter, however, young drivers in all U.S. states must adhere to a special set of laws until they've proven themselves to be capable and responsible drivers. Consult your state DMV driving manual for specific state laws.

This chapter is designed to familiarize you with basic driving skills that, when done incorrectly, may result in traffic infractions and dangerous situations. It's intended to show new drivers the proper way to handle basic driving situations.

Buckle Up

Some people complain that seatbelts are uncomfortable or that they don't really save lives. But statistics don't lie. According to a report by the National Highway Traffic Safety Administration

This young driver is taking her first driving lesson, monitored by an instructor. Notice that both driver and passenger are buckled up and wearing their safety belts.

(NHTSA), seatbelt use has steadily risen and traffic fatalities (per mile traveled) have steadily dropped since 1994.

Not only is it safer to wear a seatbelt, it's the law. Seatbelt laws differ from state to state. In some states, all occupants must wear a seatbelt at all times. Laws in other states vary, depending on the occupant's age and where he or she is sitting. New Hampshire is the only state that doesn't have seatbelt laws. Generally, all young children must wear seatbelts or have special child seats. Fines for not wearing seatbelts generally range from $10 to $50 for a first offense, although some are higher.

Speeding

Speed limit signs tell drivers when a new speed zone begins. Limits are lower in areas where it's dangerous to drive faster, such as suburban neighborhoods, school zones, and roads with curves or limited visibility. They are higher on expressways and freeways because there are fewer uncontrolled intersections and driveways connected to them. Interstate highways have the highest speed limits because they are divided highways with no intersections or driveways obstructing the flow of traffic.

Breaking the speed limit is one of the most common traffic infractions. This often happens by accident when a driver is late or when a driver simply forgets to watch how fast he or she is traveling. Sometimes, a driver will miss a speed zone sign. Impatient drivers may make a habit of driving too fast or tailgating (following other drivers too closely). Together, these practices make for very dangerous situations.

If you are driving too quickly and following too closely, you may not have time to stop your car. Many collisions are caused by speeding.

The fines for speeding vary from state to state. They may also differ based on how fast a driver is speeding and if his or her driving is considered reckless by a police officer. Reckless driving may include unsafe lane changes, failure to use a turn signal, tailgating, and excessive speed. Speeding fines may be under $100, or they could be hundreds of dollars.

Interacting with Other Drivers

In his driving manual *Safe Young Drivers: A Guide for Parents and Teens*, Phil Berardelli stresses the importance of "sharing the road." You can do this by paying attention to the drivers around you. If someone ahead of you is changing lanes or making a turn, you should "ease off" the gas and give the other driver plenty of room and time to make a move, according to Berardelli. You'll quickly realize how important this is when other drivers fail to share the road with you.

Traffic Signs, Traffic Lights, and "Right of Way"

"No Left Turn." "Yield." "Stop." "Go Slow." "Merge." These are some of the road signs that guide drivers and help keep traffic flowing. Ignoring them can result in problems for you and other drivers. You can get a ticket for running a stop sign, for example, but you can also cause a collision and harm innocent people.

Signs and traffic lights help drivers understand who goes first and who must wait their turn. Responsible drivers, however,

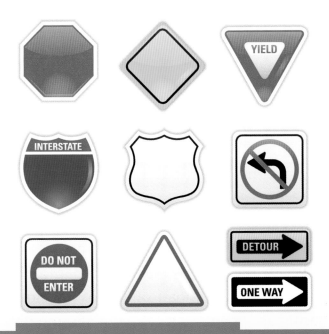

These are just a handful of the many types of traffic signs you will see when driving. Some instruct you on how to proceed, while others give you information about the road you're traveling on.

don't always rely on other drivers to follow "right of way" rules. You'll find as you begin driving that some drivers speed through red lights or fail to come to complete stops at stop signs. As a result, you need to be prepared for anything.

Changing Lanes and Passing

Changing lanes on a highway is simple and necessary. However, changing lanes without alerting other drivers beforehand may result in a dangerous situation. You can also be ticketed for failing to signal a lane change or making an unsafe lane change. To change lanes, first turn on your turn signal. Next, check your mirrors and the blind spot on the side of your car in which you plan to move. Many collisions occur when changing lanes because drivers fail to check their blind spot. When the lane is clear, turn the wheel slightly so the car moves smoothly into the next lane. Don't take too long, but don't move abruptly either.

In many instances, drivers need or want to change lanes in order to pass slower vehicles or obstructions. This is fine. Just remember the proper way to change lanes when doing so. Also, if you'll have to break the speed limit in order to pass someone, you probably shouldn't pass them. When other cars are passing you, ease off the gas to make the pass quicker and safer. Lastly, when driving on a divided highway, keep in mind that the left lane is for passing only.

Road Type	Line Type	Meaning
Two-way road	Single yellow line, broken	Passing allowed
	Double yellow lines, both solid	Passing not allowed
	Double yellow lines, one solid and one broken	Passing allowed only when driving next to the broken line
Divided highway	Broken white line	Lane changes allowed
	Solid white line	Lane changes not allowed

Intersections: Who Goes First?

There'll be times when you and one or more other drivers will approach an intersection at the same time. How you proceed depends on the specific situation. Understanding traffic lights and road signs will help you avoid confusion and collisions. Basic traffic lights have red (stop), yellow (caution or slow down), and green (go) lights. Some intersections have traffic lights that feature green or red arrows as well. In most states, it's acceptable for a driver turning right to stop at a red light, make sure the way is clear, and then make the right turn, but only if there's not a sign that says "No Turn on Red." Make sure you are familiar with how traffic lights work and the specific laws of your state and city before getting behind the wheel.

Drivers must also learn to navigate intersections that don't have traffic lights. When approaching an intersection, read the signs. If there are no signs, you don't have to stop, but you should proceed with caution. If there is a stop sign, you must come to a complete stop before proceeding. Some intersections have a yield sign. This means that you don't have to stop, but you should be especially watchful for vehicles coming from other directions. A stop sign that says "All Ways" beneath it tells you that vehicles from all directions need to stop before continuing through the intersection.

Navigating busy intersections can cause stress for young drivers. However, the rules for intersections are well defined and easy to follow. The following list will help you understand who goes first:

Busy intersections can seem complex and intimidating to young drivers. However, when drivers follow the rules of the road, intersections help safely regulate the flow of traffic.

1. A driver approaching an intersection must yield to drivers already in the intersection.
2. When two drivers approach an intersection from opposite directions, the driver turning left must yield to the driver going straight. If the light is green, you can enter the intersection in preparation of your turn.
3. When two or more drivers stop at a stop sign and they are at 90-degree angles to each other, the driver on the left must yield to the other driver.
4. When entering a roadway from a driveway, parking lot, or private road, you must yield to all traffic and pedestrians.
5. You may not enter an intersection if traffic has blocked the way out of the intersection.
6. You may not enter a traffic circle until the way is clear.

Driving Under the Influence

By now, you should know that underage drinking, excessive drinking, and doing illegal drugs are never good ideas. But getting behind the wheel of a car while intoxicated is just plain stupid. We've already discussed how irresponsible drivers can cause danger on the roads. Intoxicated drivers make it even more dangerous for themselves, their passengers, and the people with whom they share the road. You may not know it, but driving while under the influence of some prescription drugs is also against the law. Your doctor or pharmacist can tell you

Learning all the rules of the road may sound daunting, but diligence in preparing for your road test will certainly pay off in the end.

which medications are safe to take before driving and which aren't.

Laws against drunk driving differ from state to state. Punishments for drunk driving may include heavy fines, jail time, a suspended or revoked license, and community service. Repercussions for multiple offenses are usually harsher.

There are other consequences to drunk driving. Imagine what would happen if you injured or killed another person while driving drunk. Not only would you be prosecuted for your offenses, but you'd also have to live with that fact for the rest of your life. How do you think your family would feel? How do you think the victim's family would feel? Do yourself and everyone else a favor: never drive while under the influence of alcohol and drugs.

The Consequences of Breaking Traffic Laws

Nearly every experienced driver will tell you that he or she has received at least one traffic ticket. Nobody's perfect, and mistakes will happen. Responsible drivers learn from their mistakes. After all, no one wants to get a ticket and go to court.

If you're found guilty of breaking a traffic law, you will be fined. Most states also have a points system. Drivers who break the law receive points. To reduce the number of points on their license, drivers can usually attend driving school. If you accumulate too many points, your license can be suspended or revoked.

Points usually remain on a driver's record for two or more years, depending on the state.

Respect for the Police

You may one day be pulled over by the police. While this may upset you, keep your cool and talk respectfully to the officer. He or she is just doing a job and trying to keep people safe. Arguing and begging won't work, so remain calm and polite. Have your license and registration ready. And if you truly think that you're innocent, save your argument for court. Just don't forget to come prepared to plead your case.

HOW DO I DRIVE SAFELY AND RESPONSIBLY?

Ever heard of defensive driving? It's the opposite of aggressive driving. After all, the aim of defensive driving is to reduce the risk of injuries, collisions, and mishaps by being mindful of such things as the weather, road conditions, and other drivers. It's not really a driving skill—it's more like a driving philosophy.

An important part of defensive driving is courtesy for other drivers. For example, you'll find that it can be difficult to pull out of a parking lot and onto a busy street. Aggressive drivers will refuse to slow down to make it easier for you. But a defensive driver will slow down to give you enough time to join the flow of traffic. It isn't always safe to do this, but defensive drivers watch for situations where it is.

The three-second rule helps drivers tell when they are driving too close to the car in front of them. See if your parents follow this rule while riding in the car with them. First, look for a stationary object up ahead, such as a tree or a sign. When the car ahead of you passes the object, count from 1,001 to 1,003. If you pass the object before you finish, you are too close to the car ahead of you. If the driver in that car slammed on the brakes, your parents probably wouldn't have enough time to stop and would hit the car's rear bumper. Some drivers recommend using a four- or five-second rule just to be extra safe, especially in poor weather.

Avoid Distractions

Radios, cell phones and other handheld electronics, food, makeup, and even other passengers are all distractions for drivers. Looking away from the road for just three seconds to answer your cell phone, check a text message, or adjust the radio is long enough to cause a major collision. Many states have laws against talking on the phone without a hands-free headset while driving. Whether you've just earned your driver's license or you're a seasoned driver, it's always a good idea to limit diversions while driving. Avoid using iPods or GPS devices while in motion. Eat and put on your makeup before you leave the house. Ask your passengers to act responsibly while you are driving. Wait until you stop to change the radio station, pick up your phone, or check your text messages.

Driving in Bad Weather

Rain, snow, sleet, fog, and high winds can make driving difficult. Poor road conditions caused by bad weather—such as ice, standing water, and mud—can lead to problems, especially for young drivers. When driving in bad weather, turn on your headlights. Also, reduce your speed by 5 or 10 miles (8 or 16 kilometers) per hour. This will give you more time to react. Depending on the situation, you may need to reduce your speed even more. For example, snowstorms can lead to low-visibility conditions called whiteouts, which make driving nearly impossible. If you get stuck on the road in such a situation, drive slowly and cautiously, regardless of the speed of other drivers around you. Turn on your hazard lights when

Using a cell phone when driving is dangerous because it takes your attention away from the controls of the car and traffic.

driving well below the speed limit. You may actually find it necessary to stop altogether if the weather is bad enough.

What Is Road Rage?

With so many cars on the road, some people allow the stress of driving to get the better of them. Some even lash out at other drivers. These are aggressive drivers who fail to follow defensive driving techniques.

On a busy day, there could be thousands of other drivers on the road, each with their own deadlines to meet, errands to run,

Road rage is a distraction just like talking on the phone or eating while driving. Yelling at another driver instead of watching the road increases your chances of getting into a collision.

and people to see. Responsible and safe drivers must recognize this fact. Aggressive drivers, on the other hand, forget to think about their fellow drivers. They may become angry when someone changes lanes in front of them or slows down to make a turn. Road rage usually includes yelling and gesturing at other drivers. Some drivers become so angry that they exit their car and approach other drivers at stoplights. Some incidents of road rage even result in violence. When encountering aggressive drivers, it is always best to back off and let them go, rather than confronting them and escalating an already dangerous situation.

Maintaining Your Car

Safe, responsible drivers recognize the importance of basic car maintenance. This doesn't mean you need to take a class in auto repair. Maintaining a "healthy" car isn't hard when you take the time to learn how.

You should be familiar with the fluids that your car needs to run properly, how to check them, and how to replenish them. Your owner's manual will show you how to do this. Important fluids include windshield cleaner, motor oil, gasoline, transmission fluid, antifreeze, and power steering fluid. Watch for puddles beneath your vehicle, which is a sign that fluids are leaking. Bad smells and smoke are also signs of problems. Ignoring such problems can result in irreparable damage to your car.

Other areas of maintenance that you should be familiar with include air filters, sparkplugs, fuses, lights, belts, hoses, and

Many drivers choose to take their cars to a mechanic to have their brakes changed. However, with proper training, anyone can learn to change a car's brakes.

wipers. Again, you don't have to know how to repair or change all these parts, but it helps to have a basic understanding of how they function so that you know when they are malfunctioning. Changing and replacing parts like air filters and wipers is easier than you may think.

You should have your brakes inspected about every 12,000 miles (19,312 km). When brake pads begin to wear down, they usually make a scraping noise. Many brake pads are designed to squeak or chirp when they wear down so that the driver knows it's time to have them replaced. Don't ignore these signs.

Tire Maintenance

Tires can lose air pressure as time passes. Keep a tire gauge in your car, and check the pressure periodically. Tires also wear down over time. When the treads get too thin, tires won't grip the road like they used to, especially in snow, rain, mud, and other slippery situations. "Bald" tires increase the risk of collisions.

Here's a simple test you can do to see if you need new tires: insert a penny, with the president's head pointing down, into the tire tread. If you can see all of the president's head, you need new tires. Front tires wear out quicker than rear tires due to braking. To extend the life of your tires, have them rotated every 6,000 miles (9,656 km), which means the front tires are switched with the rear ones.

Flat tires can occur at any time, even when they're brand new. Knowing how to change a flat tire can mean the difference between sitting on the side of the road waiting for help and getting home on time. The first and most important step in changing a tire is having the proper tools. Always have a spare tire, a lug nut wrench, a flashlight, and a car jack in your car. Once you have the right tools, follow these steps:

1. If possible, position the car on a flat surface off the road with your hazard lights on. Apply the emergency brake. For manual transmission cars, put the car in first gear.
2. Remove the hubcap and loosen the lug nuts.

3. Use the jack to raise the car until the tire spins freely.
4. Remove the lug nuts and the flat tire.
5. Place the spare tire on the axle.
6. Hand-tighten the lug nuts.
7. Lower the jack so that the tire is firmly on the ground.
8. Use the wrench to finish tightening the lug nuts.

How Do I Jump-Start a Dead Battery?

Most drivers have had to deal with a dead battery at least once. It's not fun to come out of the mall to discover that you left your headlights on and drained the battery. Luckily, it's usually very easy to get your car started again—provided you have jumper cables and know how to use them.

You may be able to use a battery charger to energize your battery. Most of the time, however, you can use the battery in another vehicle. Jump-starting a dead battery is easy, but the cables must be correctly attached to avoid problems. Follow the directions below. If this process doesn't work, your battery is probably completely dead and should be replaced.

One last word of advice: batteries can give off hydrogen and oxygen as they charge. These gases are flammable. Keep open flames away from the battery while charging. Wear gloves and goggles if they are available.

1. Align the front of the second car close to the front of your car. Make sure the cars are not touching.
2. Open both hoods and turn off all lights and radios.

Using jumper cables to jump-start a dead battery is a simple process that all drivers should learn.

3. Attaching the cables: The following steps must be conducted in this order.

   a. Attach one clamp of a cable to the positive post on the dead battery (positive is always red).

   b. Attach the other clamp of the same cable to the positive post of the other battery.

   c. Attach one clamp of the other cable to the negative post on the live battery (negative is always black).

d. Last, attach the other clamp of the second cable to a metal part of the engine of the car that has the dead battery. Don't attach the clamp to a moving part or to the battery itself. This can cause sparks that may ignite battery fumes.

4. Start the engine of the second car and let it idle for several minutes.

5. Start your engine and let both engines idle for several minutes.

6. Carefully remove the clamps in the opposite order that you put them on.

Gearing Up

Listed below are items that you may want to keep in your car at all times. Some are more important than others:

- Spare tire
- Car jack
- Toolkit (socket wrenches, screwdrivers, etc.)
- Duct tape
- Jumper cables
- Battery charger
- Gallon of water
- Motor oil
- Antifreeze
- Windshield cleaner
- Flashlight

- Insurance and registration papers
- Owner's manual
- Emergency numbers (AAA, towing company, local police, etc.)
- Ice scraper
- Blanket
- Rags
- First-aid kit
- Emergency flares or cones
- Maps
- Tire gauge

By keeping these items handy at all times, you can ensure that you'll be prepared in any emergency.

Myths and Facts

Myth **When I'm tired, I can regain my focus by rolling down the window, drinking coffee, or turning up the radio.**

Fact: ➡ A tired driver is a dangerous driver. The best solution for sleepiness is to get some rest before continuing the trip.

 It's OK to use my horn to let other drivers know that I'm angry.

Fact: ➡ Horns should be used sparingly. They should never be used in anger. A short toot is sufficient to make another driver aware that you're in their blind spot or warn them when they're about to pull out in front of you without looking. Frequent and prolonged honking can upset and anger other drivers.

 If my car has airbags, I don't need to wear a seatbelt.

Fact: ➡ Airbags are designed to work in conjunction with seatbelts. Always wear your seatbelt when in a moving vehicle.

WHAT HAPPENS IF I HAVE A COLLISION?

According to the National Highway Traffic Safety Administration (NHTSA), traffic collisions are the leading cause of death for Americans ages fifteen to twenty (referred to as "young drivers" by the organization). The NHTSA reports that 13 percent of all drivers involved in a fatal car crash were young drivers.

These statistics are presented not to scare you away from driving but to warn you of the dangers that driving presents to teenagers. Much of the information in this chapter is based on the thorough research of the NHTSA.

Common Mistakes

While teen collisions have decreased significantly over the past decade, they are still high enough to be the leading

Police officers are trained to spot indications of intoxication, such as slurred speech, poor coordination, and hostility during sobriety tests.

cause of death for young drivers. The NHTSA's efforts to reduce teen traffic fatalities focus on three problem areas.

Lack of Experience

Studies show that young drivers are more likely to underestimate dangerous situations while driving. According to the Insurance Institute for Highway Safety (IIHS), crash rates for every mile driven are four times higher for those ages sixteen to nineteen than for older drivers. Graduated driver's license programs have helped reduce teen fatality rates, but this age group continues to be the most at risk.

No Seatbelt

Seatbelts save lives, as we have already discussed. According to the National Center for Chronic Disease Prevention and Health Promotion (NCCDPHP), teenagers are more likely than those in other age groups to neglect wearing seatbelts when someone else is driving. All drivers need to make a habit of buckling up—and insisting that their passengers do the same—every time they get behind the wheel of a car.

Alcohol

In 2007, 31 percent of young drivers killed in automobile collisions had a blood alcohol concentration (BAC) of .01 grams per deciliter (g/dL) or higher. Twenty-six percent had a BAC of .08 or higher, which in most states is the level at which a driver is considered legally impaired. Organizations like Mothers Against Drunk Driving (MADD) and Students Against

Destructive Decisions (SADD) have done a lot to educate others about the dangers of driving while intoxicated. But teens continue to die every year due to drunk driving. Be smart—never drink and drive.

After the Crash

If and when a collision occurs, you may have the urge to panic. You may feel angry or frightened, but it's very important to remain calm. Your actions in the moments that follow a collision will require a level head.

It's illegal and irresponsible to leave the scene of a collision. So don't think about fleeing, particularly if the collision is your fault. If possible, pull off to a safe area to assess the damage. If it's unsafe to exit your vehicle, or if you can't exit your vehicle, stay where you are and wait for help.

If you have them, use road flares or orange cones to alert other drivers. Make sure you and everyone else involved in the collision are safe. Be mindful of other motorists and pedestrians who may be in the vicinity. Call 911 if necessary. Calmly tell the dispatcher your name, where the collision occurred, and what happened.

Stay on the line until help arrives or the dispatcher tells you to hang up. A dispatcher will also send the police to the scene of the collision if you need a mediator. Oftentimes, however, the police aren't required to report to a collision scene, especially if there are no injuries and all vehicles involved can be driven away.

Road flares burn very brightly and are visible from a great distance, day or night. The flame is very hot, however, so take caution when using them, and never use them for fun.

Injuries

Auto collision injuries can range from aches and pains to life-threatening wounds. Seatbelts and airbags are designed to save your life in case of a collision, but they can cause injuries, too. Many people have bruises from their seatbelts after a collision. The force created by an inflated airbag has been shown to cause injuries as well. Concussions and whiplash are two more common auto collision injuries. If anyone involved in the crash doesn't feel 100 percent OK, call 911.

Exchange Driver Information

Once you've assessed the situation, the drivers involved need to talk and exchange driver information. Ask to see the other drivers' licenses and insurance information, and write down names, addresses, phone numbers, insurance companies, and insurance policy numbers. Also write down the year, make, model, and license plate numbers of any cars involved in the collision. If a police officer is present, record his or her name and the police report number. Takes notes regarding the collision itself, and take photos if possible.

Some drivers involved in a collision may try to bully their way out of blame. Others may try to give false information, or simply leave without following the steps covered in this section. In these cases, contact the police. Don't get into an argument with another driver, but don't let him or her take advantage of you either. Also, insurance companies will advise you not to admit blame to a police officer. Rather, let the police be the judge after

The sight of your damaged car can make you depressed or angry, but always remember that cars can be fixed or replaced. It is more important to make sure everyone involved walks away safe and sound.

hearing both sides of the story. Keep in mind that the calmer you are, the easier it'll be to plead your case.

Need a Lift?

If your vehicle is not drivable, you will need to call a tow truck. Many drivers pay for membership in the American Automobile Association (AAA). This membership entitles you to a wide range of roadside services, including towing. The police may contact a tow truck service for you, or you may have to do it yourself. However, towing services can be costly, and an AAA membership is a good thing to have in case of an emergency.

What Happens Next?

After a collision, drivers should report the incident to their insurance companies. (In most states, if you get into a collision without insurance, your license will be suspended.) What happens next depends on who's at fault. The insurance company of the person at fault generally pays for the damages. Sometimes, both drivers are equally responsible, and their respective insurance companies cover their damages.

Insurance holders often have a deductible—an amount you must pay toward a claim before your insurance pays. For example, if the damages to your car come to $1,000 and you have a $200 deductible, the insurance company will give you $800 toward fixing your car.

The price you pay for car insurance is called the premium. Premiums are high or low depending on the type of insurance you get. For instance, some types cover injuries and collisions, while others just cover collisions. Premiums are also affected by the type of driver you are. Teenage drivers naturally have higher insurance rates because they're considered a higher risk. Teen boys have the highest premiums. Depending on the severity of the collision and your previous driving record, your insurance premiums may go up.

In addition to insurance issues, you may also have legal issues to deal with. For example, if a police officer determines that you caused the collision because you failed to properly signal your lane change, you may be issued a ticket. A reckless driver who causes injuries or fatalities may even have to serve time in jail.

Hit the Road

Collisions happen. Even the safest and most responsible drivers have them. Chances are if you ask your parents or older siblings, they may have a story or two for you. While there are no guarantees that you'll never have a car collision, you can drastically reduce your chances of having one by becoming a defensive driver.

accelerator The pedal on a car that gives the engine gas and moves the car forward.

conscientious The act of paying great care and attention to detail.

cruise control A technological function in some cars that maintains a constant speed without having to use the gas pedal.

divided highway A highway that has a middle barrier or grassy median separating the lanes going in opposite directions.

fatality A death resulting from a collision.

graduated Divided in steps or stages.

infraction Failure to obey a law.

intoxicated To be affected by alcohol or drugs.

malfunction To fail to function properly.

maneuver A controlled change of course of a vehicle.

merge To blend gradually into traffic.

navigate To find a way through or to a place.

obstruction Something that causes or forms a blockage in the way.

occupant A person in a vehicle.

parallel Relating to two things that are the same distance apart at all points.

pedestrian Someone traveling on foot.

permit An official document granting permission for something.

privilege Permission to do something that is not granted to everyone.

restriction Something that limits or controls something or someone else.

revoke To take something away that has officially been given to someone.

simulation A computer program or game that simulates a real activity, such as driving.

violation A crime or a breaking of the rules.

American Automobile Association (AAA)
1000 AAA Drive
Heathrow, FL 32746
(407) 444-7000
Web site: http://www.aaa.com
   The American Automobile Association provides its
   members with emergency services, travel directions,
   maps, car buying tips, and more.

Governors Highway Safety Association (GHSA)
750 First Street NE, Suite 720
Washington, DC 20002
(202) 789-0942
Web site: http://www.ghsa.org
   The GHSA is a nonprofit organization representing
   the highway safety offices of all U.S. states and
   territories. Its mission is "to improve traffic safety,
   influence national policy, and enhance program
   management."

Insurance Institute for Highway Safety (IIHS)
1005 N. Glebe Road, Suite 800
Arlington, VA 22201
(703) 247-1500

Web site: http://www.iihs.org

The IIHS is a nonprofit, scientific, educational organization dedicated to reducing deaths, injuries, and property damage from crashes on U.S. highways.

Mothers Against Drunk Driving (MADD)
511 E. John Carpenter Freeway, Suite 700
Irving, TX 75062
(800) 438-6233
Web site: http://www.madd.org

The mission of MADD is to stop drunk driving, support the victims of drunk driving, and prevent underage drinking.

National Highway Traffic Safety Association (NHTSA)
1200 New Jersey Avenue SE
West Building
Washington, DC 20590
(888) 327-4236
Web site: http://www.nhtsa.dot.gov

An agency of the U.S. Department of Transportation, the NHTSA is dedicated to saving lives, preventing injuries, and reducing vehicle-related crashes.

Students Against Destructive Decisions (SADD)
255 Main Street
Marlborough, MA 01752
(877) SADD-INC (723-3462)

Web site: http://www.sadd.org

SADD strives to provide students with the best prevention tools possible to deal with the issues of underage drinking, drug use, impaired driving, and other destructive decisions.

Web Sites

Due to the changing nature of Internet links, Rosen Publishing has developed an online list of Web sites related to the subject of this book. This site is updated regularly. Please use this link to access this list:

http://www.rosenlinks.com/faq/driv

For Further Reading

Aksomitis, Linda, ed. *Teen Driving*. Farmington Hills, MI: Greenhaven Press, 2008.

Berardelli, Phil. *Safe Young Drivers: A Guide for Parents and Teens*. Mountain Lake Park, MD: Mountain Lake Press, 2008.

Cefrey, Holly. *Frequently Asked Questions About Drinking and Driving*. New York, NY: Rosen Publishing Group, Inc., 2008.

Gerdes, Louise I. *Teen Driving*. Farmington Hills, MI: Greenhaven Press, 2008.

Gravelle, Karen. *The Driving Book: Everything New Drivers Need to Know but Don't Know to Ask*. New York, NY: Walker and Company, 2005.

Scotti, Anthony J. *Driving Techniques: For the Professional and Non-Professional*. Palm Coast, FL: PhotoGraphics Publishing, 2004.

Van Tuyl, Christine. *Drunk Driving*. Farmington Hills, MI: Greenhaven Press, 2006.

Index

About the Author

Greg Roza has written and edited educational materials for children for the past eight years. He has a master's degree in English from the State University of New York at Fredonia. He lives in Hamburg, New York, with his wife, Abigail, and his three children, Autumn, Lincoln, and Daisy—each of whom will receive driving lessons from Roza himself. He has a clean driving record.

Photo Credits

Cover © www.istockphoto.com/Cristian Lazzari; p. 6 © Robyn Beck/Getty Images; p. 8 © David Young-Wolff/Photo Edit; p. 10 © www.istockphoto.com/Gene Chutka; p. 13 © www.istockphoto.com/Brian Jackson; pp. 15, 18, 23, 40 © www.istockphoto.com/Lisa F. Young; p. 20 © AP Photos; p. 25 © www.istockphoto.com/Jeff Giniewicz; p. 27 © © www.istockphoto.com; p. 30 © Bob Daemmrich/The Image Works; p. 32 © www.istockphoto.com/Gene Chutka; p. 37 © www.istockphoto.com/Marty Heitner; p. 38 © www.istockphoto.com/Kirk Johnson; p. 43 © David R. Frazier/Photo Researchers; p. 48 © www.istockphoto.com/Wayne Howard; p. 51 © www.istockphoto.com/Joseph Justice; p. 53 © www.istockphoto.com/Don Bayley.

Designer: Nicole Russo; Editor: Nicholas Croce;
Photo Researcher: Marty Levick